TO WHOM IT MAY CONCERN

FREDERIK SWENNEN

Essay on
Public Private Partnerships on
Cultural Heritage

TO WHOM
IT MAY
CONCERN

UPA

This essay is a shot across the bow of
public and private actors, encouraging
them to show their colours on public private
partnerships (PPP) on cultural heritage.
Encounters between public and private
partners on cultural heritage have not yet
come of age; as such, an exploration into the
means to develop the current one-way shifts
of resources between public and private
actors towards full-grown PPP-projects is
necessary.

This essay contains a short exploration from
a legal and a managerial perspective, and
focuses on art collections, art storage and
artists' archives as representative examples
of creative entrepreneurship in the field of
movable cultural heritage. It concludes that
after both public and private partners have
reached the right mindset, tax and legal
measures must be improved to serve as
leverage for PPP projects.

/ TABLE OF CONTENTS

contents

TECHNIQUES

ILLUSTRATIONS

/ INTRODUCTION

/ INTRODUCTION

NOTES

1
The Dutch Boekmanstichting
can already boast some
accomplishments: J. BANK, *Stads
mecenaat en lokale overheid*,
Amsterdam, Boekmanstudies,
1999; I. JANSSEN and T.
GUBBELS, *Bedrijvige musea.
Private betrokkenheid in de
praktijk*, Stichting DOEN/
Mondriaan Stichting/Stichting
Boekmanstudies, Amsterdam,
2003;C. BLOTKAMP, *In loving
memory. Van particuliere collectie
naar museum*, Amsterdam/
The Hague, Boekmanstudies/
Vereniging Rembrandt, 2008; I.
VAN HAMERSVELD and T. GUBBELS,
*Bondgenoten of tegenpolen?
Samenwerking tussen
kunstverzamelaars in Nederland*,
Amsterdam/The Hague,
Boekmanstudies/Vereniging
Rembrandt, 2010.

2
F. SWENNEN, "Deconstructing
– Reconstructing. PPP
of Contemporary Arts
Organisations", www.bamart.be
> EN > Topics > Documentation
(Report of an Art Brussels 2010
Debate); Agentschap Kunsten
en Erfgoed, *Over collecties*,
Brussels, 2010; P. DEPONDT, *Met
nieuwsgierige blik*, Brussels,
ASP Editions, 2010. In April
2011, Mu.ZEE will publish the
proceedings and the catalogue of
its *Public Private Paintings*-project.

Antwerp was covered in snow, when experts from around Europe convened for an expert seminar on *public private partnerships on cultural heritage* on 21 December 2010. The seminar was hosted by prof. dr. Frederik SWENNEN (research unit Citizens and the Law, University of Antwerp Law Research School) and prof. dr. Annick SCHRAMME (coordinator, master in cultural management, department of cultural management, University of Antwerp).

For the first time in Flanders,[1] all stakeholders entered into an academic discussion on the opportunities and dangers of collaborating on cultural heritage. *Academics* from both law and (cultural) management faculties guided the interdisciplinary discussion. Policy makers from different levels and directors of publicly funded museums and arts organisations represented the *public sector*. Those invited for the *private sector* were committed collectors, artists ('estates' representatives) and captains of industry. The expert seminar hence was complementary to other initiatives on the same theme.[2]

The seminar was built around three power sessions, each with an introduction by an academic, and complemented with a round table discussion. The keynote lecture, which served as a basis for the first power session, was held by prof. dr. dr. h.c. mult. Bruno S. FREY, with reflections in his capacity as a *cultural economist*. A second session concerned the *legal techniques* for PPP on cultural heritage, which was introduced by prof. dr. Anne Mie DRAYE. Prof. dr. Sigrid HEMELS finally addressed tax incentives to enhance private patronage in a session on *tax instruments*.

What follows is a report of the seminar in the form of an
essay with reflections, on the basis of the introductions and
the interventions by the participants.* I will first address the
general context of PPP and of economic and legal aspects
of cultural heritage. Then I will briefly discuss the possible
fields of application of PPP on cultural heritage. Finally,
I will review the legal and tax techniques of PPP, before
concluding.

*

The seminar was recorded entirely for scientific purposes

A — PPP

/ GENERAL
CONTEXT

B — CULTURAL HERITAGE,
LAW AND
ECONOMICS

A — PPP

NOTES

3
Definition of PPP by the Flemish
PPP Knowledge Centre,
www.kenniscentrumpps.be

4
Interventions by Fernand Huts and
An Moons.

5
K. Van Gestel, J. Voets & K.
Verhoest, Samen in bad? PPS
bij gemeentelijke zwembaden.
Beleidsvoorbereidend rapport,
Steunpunt Bestuurlijke Organisatie
Vlaanderen, Brussels, 2009, p. 15.

6
Design, Build,
Finance & Maintain.

7
Design, Build,
Finance & Operate.

8
Keynote lecture
Bruno S. Frey.

9
Intervention by Ivo Van
Vaerenbergh.

The Flemish Decree of 18 July 2003 on PPP defines PPP projects as *projects that are carried out by public and private parties jointly and in a partnership in order to create a value-added for those parties* (s. 2, 1°).

Public parties are broadly defined as both public authorities and private parties under the financial or managerial control of public authorities (s. 2, 5°).

Private parties are any other parties than public parties; for the purpose of this essay both individuals and corporations may qualify as private parties.

Consequently, the mere shift of resources from public to private parties (e.g. information, subventions) or vice versa (e.g. donations, management/marketing techniques) does not qualify as PPP: a project must be carried out jointly and in a partnership. Each party thus preserves its own identity and responsibilities.

Besides, PPP may not consist of shifting all risks, charges etc. to one party and all benefits to the other.

The partnership must create an added value for both parties, on a financial, societal or operational level,[3] as it were a return on investment.

PPP must also be distinguished from mixed financing techniques that do not imply a project being carried out jointly by both public and private partners.[4]

PPP is achieved via various forms and techniques.[5]
According to its *object*, a distinction may be made
between object-related PPP (e.g. infrastructure) and area
development.
According to its *form*, one distinguishes between
contractual PPP and participative PPP, where a new
(legal) structure is set up in which all parties participate.
In practice many hybrid forms of PPP occur. PPP anyhow
may not be reduced to DBFM[6] or DBFO[7]-projects on
infrastructure.

———————

PPP encounters many objections of both economic
and legal nature, from both the public and the private
perspectives. Such objections are mostly based on
approaching the public and private actors as opposites,
striving for fundamentally different goals, rather than as a
continuum in the free market economy. The public sector
is considered only to strive for the common good in the
long term, thus offering durability to all its stakeholders.
Yet, it is associated with missing incentives, overregulation,
bureaucracy leading to irresponsibility and a lack of
flexibility. The private sector is suspected only to use its
flexibility with a view to short-term profitability and self-
interest.

One major pitfall of PPP is that it will only strengthen
the flaws on both sides, with each side exonerating its
responsibility.[8]
On the public side, the lack of incentives for the operators,
inflexibility in decision-making and diffused responsibility
seem to be the major flaws. According to some private
parties, overregulation of governance in public services
results in too little flexibility in negotiating a deal. This was
easier in the past.[9]
On the private side, positive externalities and equal
distribution would not be taken into account.
In-between, the multi-levelled organisation of public

authorities may be a negotiation disadvantage vis-à-vis the private market when it comes to PPP agreements.

The aim of PPP is, however, to combine the strengths of both sides so as to overcome market failure, by incorporating common good and use value of the market.[10] PPP will thus be set up as a mutually supportive project with divided responsibility, where incentives for operators and flexibility are used to reach fair goals.
Yet goals and roles of all partners need to be well defined from the beginning.[11]
For some entrepreneurs,[12] PPP may thus serve to unlock the potential in human and other assets, such as cultural heritage, that is currently blocked in the public sector.
A market approach may be useful in this regard – albeit of course that a return on private investments should be realised. For the public sector, it is important that the accountability of the public authorities may not be haggled over.

NOTES

10
R.C. READY and S. NAVRUD, "Why value cultural heritage?" in S. NAVRUD & R.C. READY (eds.), Valuing Cultural Heritage, Edward Elgar Publishing, 2002, p. 7.

11
Intervention by
An MOONS.

12
Intervention by
Fernand HUTS.

13
D. LOWENTHAL, The Past is a Foreign Country, New York, Cambridge University Press, 1985.

14
J.H. MERRYMAN, A.E.ELSEN and S.K. URICE, Law, Ethics and the Visual Arts, Kluwer Law International, Alphen a/d Rijn, 2007, 1141.

15
For the Association of Cultural Economics International: www. culturaleconomics.org

16
A. KLAMER, [Lecture 22 February 2010], in Agentschap Kunsten en Erfgoed, Over collecties, Brussels, 2010, p. 13.

17
In general on valuation methods for public goods: A. VEKEMAN et al., "Economische aspecten van cultuur en sport", in J. LIEVENS and H. WAEGE, Participatie in Vlaanderen 1, Leuven, Acco academic, 2011, p. 223 ff

18
R.C. READY and S. NAVRUD, "Why value cultural heritage?" in S. NAVRUD & R.C. READY (eds.), Valuing Cultural Heritage, Edward Elgar Publishing, 2002, p. 3-4.

19
A. VEKEMAN et al., "De niet-gebruikswaarde bij waardering van cultuur en sport", in J. LIEVENS and H. WAEGE, Participatie in Vlaanderen 2, Leuven, Acco academic, 2011, p. 375 ff, with a case study for the Stedelijk Museum voor Actuele Kunst, Ghent.

20
R. MASON, "Assessing Values in Conservation Planning: Methodological Issues and Choices", in M. DE LA TORRE (ed.), Assessing the Values of Cultural Heritage, The Getty Conservation Institute Research Report, 2002, p. 13.

B — CULTURAL HERITAGE, LAW AND ECONOMICS

Cultural heritage is the legacy of tangible and intangible attributes of a group or society that are selected from the past, inherited, maintained in the present and bestowed for the benefit of future generations. Physical or tangible cultural heritage can be immovable (including historical buildings or monuments), or movable (including artefacts). Aspects of a particular culture, maintained by social customs during a specific period in history are considered intangible cultural heritage. This includes social values and traditions, customs, and practices, aesthetic and spiritual beliefs, artistic expressions, language and other aspects of human activity.[13] The word 'heritage' itself indicates that we inherited our cultural heritage over the centuries, during which a selective accumulation took place.[14]

From a cultural economic perspective,[15] cultural heritage will traditionally be considered a *public good*, as opposed to private goods.[16] Public goods have specific characteristics regarding both their use and non-use value.[17]
Regarding use value, it is characteristic for a public good that its consumption is non-excludable and non-rival.[18] This means that no one can be excluded from enjoying the good and that several persons can enjoy it simultaneously. Besides, public goods also have a large non-use value, particularly an existence value and a bequest value.[19]
In between use value and non-use value, the option value reflects the preservation of possible future consumption by a consumer.[20] This is an important positive externality of all public goods.

Both by the nature of their use value (consumption) and of their non-use value, public goods, however, cause market failure. Because of this market failure, the traditional conclusion in economics is that cultural heritage should be supplied, i.e. owned and operated, by public authorities.

Public authorities of all levels intervene in the supply of cultural goods. Three main levels may be distinguished: the global/international, the national, and the regional/local. The principles of multi-level governance apply. From an economic point of view, policy instruments – and the revenue to implement them – should exist at all levels so as to regulate and fund the supply of cultural goods. To develop a policy at the lowest possible level allows the necessary made-to-measure work. The multiplicity of approaches towards cultural heritage at different levels may broaden the supply of cultural goods to the public. Nonetheless, the multi-levelled organisation can also complicate decision-making where different levels are concerned.[21]

When analysing public supply of cultural goods, it is necessary to consider the different actors with their different roles, from the public in general, via interest groups, politicians in the executive or the legislative and finally the officials implementing the policy.[22]

There is, however, a more modern economic view on cultural heritage[23] that considers public goods and private goods as the extremes of a continuum, and focuses on what happens in between.[24]

Many goods indeed unite a mix of *characteristics* of both public and private goods. Moreover, one could intervene by applying characteristics of a private good to a public good, e.g. by controlling consumption value through limited accessibility of a site with (differentiated) admission charges. Preservation of heritage might be a reason for such an intervention. The public good characteristics may thus be reduced – though not excluded.

21
Intervention
by Fernand HUTS.

22
Bruno S. FREY in his
keynote lecture.

23
Presented by Bruno S. FREY in his
keynote lecture. Cf also B.S. FREY,
*Arts & Economics. Analysis and
Cultural Policy*, 2nd Ed., Berlin,
Springer Verlag, 2003; A. PEACOCK
& I. RIZZO, *The Heritage Game.
Economic, Policy and Practice*,
Oxford University Press, 2008.

24
Comp. P. VAN ROSSEM, "Meer
museum worden: van retrospectief
naar retroactief", *<H>ART* 36
(2008).

25
As explained
by Bruno S. FREY.

26
Bruno S. FREY explained the
different shifts in the following
scheme:

		OWNERSHIP	
		PUBLIC	PRIVATE
OPERATION	PUBLIC		
	PRIVATE		

27
www.schoenbrunn.at

28
www.fortnapoleon.be

Besides the characteristics, also the *provision* of heritage
by public authorities solely and not by the private market
may be considered as the extremes of a continuum.
A significant proportion of cultural heritage is offered on
the private market, by individuals and corporations – each
according to their different rules on (personal or corporate)
governance. A clear example is the consumption of heritage
in Venice.[25]
More importantly one should focus on the intermediate
providers, who are not typically public or private providers.
Indeed, in between the private and the public sectors,
many not-for-profit corporations and non-governmental
organisations already provide for cultural heritage.

To approach the supply of cultural goods as a
continuum, allows to better manage the instruments of
interaction between the public and the private regarding
ownership on the one hand and operation on the other.[26]
The traditional model of publicly owned *and* operated
cultural goods may thus be abandoned in preference to
other models, by shifting responsibilities from one party to
another. In Flanders, a legal framework for this is offered
by the Decree of 18 July 2003 on PPP (mentioned earlier),
which allows flexible decision-making on real estate that
belongs to the private or even the public domain of the
public authorities (s. 9 et seq.) and on participations
in private law structures (s. 14), in case a project is
recognised as a Flemish or local PPP project.

E.g. Schloss Schönbrunn in Vienna[27] is publicly owned,
but the operation is outsourced to a private for-profit
corporation, which has led to a much greater efficiency and
even profit.

Another example is Fort Napoleon in Ostend, owned
by the Flemish authorities and operated by the not-for-
profit organisation *Erfgoed Vlaanderen*; this operation is
partly outsourced to the City of Ostend, for the heritage
functions, and to a private party, for conference and
catering functions.[28]

There are also bad examples of publicly owned museums and cultural heritage sites whose operation was outsourced, which resulted either in taking the direction of recreation rather than culture,[29] or in closing down for not reaching the profit targets set out by the private partner.[30] It is debatable whether recreation on heritage sites should be rejected altogether.[31]

Outsourcing may also be limited to only some aspects of the operation.

Besides, the public authorities may choose to shift ownership from the private to the public, e.g. through favourable treatment of payment of (succession or other) taxes with cultural goods.

More rarely, privately owned heritage may be operated by the public sector.

Private-private partnerships also exist, e.g. in the operating by the National Trust[32] in England of sites owned by other private parties.

_____

Many other possible instruments of interaction between the public and the private are less far-reaching than *shifting* ownership or operation of cultural goods, but tend to only *modulate* such ownership and operation. These instruments allow the public authorities to organise their responsibility for both publicly and privately owned heritage. The duty of care for cultural heritage is a particular responsibility of public authorities on the three levels mentioned above. The consumption and option value of the cultural goods we have inherited must indeed be safeguarded for both the current and future generations.

NOTES

29
Cp the PPP project Land van Ooit Tongeren, set up as a recreational evocation of the Roman history of the city of Tongeren, but now bankrupt.

30
E.g. P. GROENENDIJK, *Rijkswerf Willemsoord. Transformatie van een industrieel monument*, Rotterdam, Uitgeverij 010, 2008.

31
Interventions by Bruno S. FREY and Kit VAN GESTEL.

32
www.nationaltrust.org.uk

33
www.unesco.org/culture

34
J. CLAIR, "Des beaux-arts considérés comme un assassinat" (Lecture for the Fonds voor Cultuurmanagement), p. 9 ff, www.deburen.eu > EN > Events > Lectures > 26 October 2010 and www. fondsvoorcultuurmanagement.be.

35
Daniel 5, 1-30

36
Interventions by Bruno S. Frey
and Anne Mie Draye.

37
No, according to J. Clair,
"Des beaux-arts considérés
comme un assassinat"
(Lecture for the Fonds voor
Cultuurmanagement), p.
11, www.deburen.eu > EN
> Events > Lectures > 26
October 2010 and www.
fondsvoorcultuurmanagement.
be.

A first way for the public authorities of fulfilling their duty of care is to provide information and 'caring' techniques free of charge to all owners of cultural goods.[33]

More important instruments are legal and tax regulations, which I will discuss in paragraph 4.
Tangible and intangible, movable and immovable, publicly and privately owned cultural heritage, including archives and libraries, is regulated by a mosaic of instruments. The public authorities will use these instruments to influence characteristics and provision of the privately owned cultural goods.
Here also, extremes should always be avoided. On the one hand, overregulation must not lead privately owned cultural goods to be perceived as publicly owned and operated. On the other hand, privatisation should not lead to an excessive commercialisation of cultural heritage. In this regard, Jean Clair drew an interesting parallel between contemporary art and the toxic assets leading to the 2007-2010 financial crisis,[34] relating contemporary art projects in fine arts museums with the MANE, THECEL, PHARES after King Belshazzar's profane banquet.[35]

It is of course debatable at which point the ideal balance between market concerns and public concerns lies. As mentioned above, the question arises, for instance, to what extent, if any, culture and education may be supplemented or even substituted with recreation. In line with concerns about education, there is the issue of authenticity: can a replica, such as Lascaux II, fulfil the functions of a public good?[36] Building replicas has been proposed for other heritage sites, too, with a view to reconciling preservation of the site with accessibility to the public. Yet could one expect from a public for culture that it settles for a facsimile of Veronese's The Wedding at Cana in its original environment of San Maggiore in Venice rather than for the original, damaged, painting in the Louvre?[37]

A — IMMOVABLE
HERITAGE

/ EXPLORING NEW OPPORTUNITIES FOR PPP ON CULTURAL HERITAGE

B — MOVABLE
HERITAGE

A — IMMOVABLE
HERITAGE

NOTES

38
http://www.culture.gouv.fr/
culture/actualites/communiq/
albanel/artpalaistokyo.html

39
Cf the description of
the projects on www.
kenniscentrumpps.be

Flanders has some experience with object-related
PPP projects regarding schools and hospitals. Also, area
development projects have been carried out.
In contrast to this general experience, there is only limited
experience with PPP on immovable cultural heritage, such
as monuments, or reusing historical or religious buildings
as stores, hotels, etc. An overview of the issues that may
arise in this regard was presented on the occasion of the
development of the Parisian Palais de Tokyo West Wing by
Olivier Kaeppelin.[38]
Until now, in Flanders no PPP projects have been
recognised as such that only or mainly concern cultural
heritage sites. Nonetheless, cultural heritage protection is
indirectly at stake in some of the officially recognised PPP
projects.[39]

The project 's Hertogenmolens was a contractual PPP
project with a view to urban development. It implied
restoration by the private party of old watermills on
the waterway the Demer, owned by the Flemish public
company Waterwegen en Zeekanaal NV. In return, a
hotel and catering exploitation was outsourced to the
private party for a period of 99 years. Moreover, the city
of Aarschot was implied in the project and granted the
private partner the right to build a mixed social-residential
housing project on land owned by the city. The mills are
not exploited as a heritage site, but are protected as a
monument.

In the city of Mechelen, a former brewery was incorporated in an urban development project. Private project developers realised the restoration of the brewery and built new units for both commercial and residential use. The brewery building is now owned by the city of Mechelen. Hotel exploitation, conference centre and catering services are outsourced. Besides, the brewery houses the city's heritage centre with a social function.

Another urban development project concerned a mill tower in Bruges that was restored and extended by a private project developer who realised 50 residential units in a contractual PPP. The city of Bruges and an inter-municipal association were the public partners, as owners of the land. The mill is not exploited as a heritage site and is not protected as a monument.

Other projects that have been carried out or are still in the pipeline concern a former power station, mills and former mine sites.

With almost no exception, the PPP projects mentioned above implied partly new destinations for the heritage concerned (hotel, catering, conference) and, more importantly, the realisation of new(ly built) units for residential or commercial use, which rendered the projects highly profitable for the private partner. In some cases, an additional public actor – owner of nearby land – was involved to that end. The profits from the project development constitute the return on investment for the private partners; it is easy to realise such return on large-scale real estate projects. It is, of course, a condition for the commitment of private partners to the restoration of the heritage site itself. Sometimes, it seems difficult, however, to find the right balance between preserving the site in its original setting, and combining it with newly-built wings.

Characteristic, too, for PPP regarding immovable cultural heritage is the active role taken by not-for-profit heritage associations[40] that operate in between the public and the private, and that are largely supported by public authorities. Furthermore, the King Baudouin Foundation serves as a knowledge centre, offering managerial services, and as a fund with a view to stimulating private initiatives in preserving heritage. This may be achieved through its generic Cultural Heritage Fund or with a specific Named Fund.

NOTES

40
Three organisations will merge into one following the example of the National Trust:
Forum voor Erfgoedverenigingen (www.onroerenderfgoed.be), which is the umbrella organisation for the local heritage organisations and serves as an interest group and single contact for the authorities.
Erfgoed Vlaanderen (www.toekomstvooronsverleden.be), is comparable to the National Trust. It operates threatened monuments and heritage sites so as to preserve them.
Open Monumentendag Vlaanderen (www.openmonumenten.be) organises the European Heritage Days (www.ehd.coe.int), a joint initiative of the Council of Europe and the European Commission, in Flanders.
A fourth association is MonumentenwachtVlaanderen (www.monumentenwacht.be), which focuses on preventive conservation of both immovable and movable heritage.

41
www.wiels.org

42
Intervention by Dirk SNAUWAERT.

B — MOVABLE HERITAGE

CONTEXT

I will now proceed to show that both characteristics of PPP on movable heritage, mentioned above, do not apply (to the same extent) to movable heritage. This partly explains why PPP on movable heritage is still largely virgin territory. However, it might be possible to create new opportunities.

As opposed to projects on immovable heritage, it is not obvious to create a return on investment for private partners with new destinations or expansions of the cultural goods.

In the operation of a movable heritage or arts organisation, a distinction may be made between the 'hardware' – or building – and the 'software' – or heritage or arts activities. The dynamics of developing hardware and software are quite different and presuppose a specific approach. The development of the Brussels contemporary art institution Wiels[41] was addressed that way.[42] The infrastructure was distinguished as a heritage landmark. Other partners, in other forms, independently develop the operational outcome.

At first sight, neither the hardware nor the software seems suitable for PPP.
Only to a limited extent can a return on investment be realised on the *infrastructure* for movable heritage or an arts organisation, because any other destination must be reconcilable with its primary cultural destination. Outsourcing catering services will hardly suffice. PPP will

only create a win-win in case a larger return on investment may be realised. One may refer in this regard to the discussion on the MoMA transaction: the sale of the vertical property right resulted in the adding of a 44-store building with apartments to one of the MoMA-wings.[43]

Even more difficult is PPP on the software, viz. *publicly owned cultural goods* or the operation of a public arts organisation. One option that seems underused is cession or licensing contracts on the intellectual property rights held by the public party.

Secondly, with regard to popular art, venture capital may be attracted through private equity funds[44] or various forms of crowd funding.[45]

Participation of private partners in the operation of heritage or arts organisations often takes the eventual form of sponsorship or financial patronage.[46] However, concerns may arise regarding influence on the decision-making process of the operation in case the organisation becomes too dependent upon private support. Mainstream would gain over avant-garde.[47] There is a risk of conflicts of interests in case a private collector-patron were to be on the board of a museum.[48] There are also some bad examples of collectors imposing Trojan Horse-like conditions on a museum[49] or withdrawing a loan unexpectedly after having realised an added value by loaning to a renowned museum. In summary, the economic acceptability for private partners on the one hand, and ethical acceptability for the public partners on the other, may prevent PPP projects to be developed on publicly owned cultural goods or public arts organisations.

In light of the insufficient means for ownership and operation of publicly owned cultural goods, even fewer means are available for PPP projects on *privately owned cultural goods*. It seems that private owners who want to publicly unlock their collection by donating it, must additionally provide the operating budget to make that possible.[50]

NOTES

43
J.H. Merryman, A.E.Elsen and S.K. Urice, *Law, Ethics and the Visual arts*, Kluwer Law International, Alphen a/d Rijn, 2007, 1190.

44
E.g. www.cultuurinvest.be

45
E.g. www.akamusic.com

46
For a historical perspective: M. Garber, *Patronizing the Arts*, Princeton University Press, 2008. The boundaries between patronage and sponsorship are not always clear: F. Grapperhaus and S. Hemels, *Mecenaat en fiscus*, Deventer, Kluwer, 2010, p. 33.

47
Cf K. Strubbe, "Het gat in onzecultuur", column in De Standaard 7 February 2011, www.standaard.be and the response by M. Reynebeau, "Speciaal in kunstland", column in De Standaard 9 February 2011, www.standaard.be.

48
E.g. L. Yablonsky, "Controversy over New Museum's plans to show trustee's collection", *The Art Newspaper* # 207, 2009.

49
E.g. District Court Brussels 13 June 1997, *Revue du notariatbelge* 1998, p. 67 (on the bequest of works by the Belgian painter Paul Maas (1890-1962)).

50
E.g. 75,000 € for a Named Fund in the King Baudouin Foundation.

51
www.weserburg.de

52
www.museiciviciveneziani.it

53
A. M. Draye, *De bescherming van het roerend en onroerend erfgoed*, Brussel, Larcier, 2007, 435 p.

54
R. Steenbergen, *De Nieuwe Mecenas*, Amsterdam, Business Contact, 2008, p. 42-44.

Some Belgian collectors were already involved in successful foreign PPP-projects on privately owned cultural goods. Before the creation of its own space in Brussels, the Vanhaerents Art Collection was partly integrated in the German 'collector's museum' NeuesMuseumWeserburg in Bremen. The building is owned by the municipality of Bremen.[51] The city, the Kunstverein Bremen and some collectors then founded the museum, whose collection exclusively consists of privately owned objects. More recently, the Belgian Vervoordt Foundation collaborates with the Fondazione Musei Civici di Venezia in a PPP-project with regard to the operation of the Palazzo Fortuny.[52] Both the collections of the Vervoordt Foundation and the Palazzo Fortuny serve as a basis for the operation, with shared curatorial views.

The described disadvantaged position of movable heritage is often explained by reference to the lack of an appropriate legislative framework. A first act on the protection of movable heritage of 1931 in fact never entered into force in the absence of an implementing Royal Decree. The two most important legislative milestones on movable heritage date from 1985 and 2003 respectively.[53] However, one must not forget that legislation is only an instrument to achieve goals that lie elsewhere.

It is more plausible to argue that potential private patrons – individual or corporate – are not committed to culture because there is no bond with the organisations rather than because there is no legislative framework.
Awareness of the functions of cultural heritage must first be raised before a patron may become committed to a project. In other words: a culture of giving presupposes a culture of asking,[54] or more generally: of appealing. Only after such culture has come into existence, can one think of accompanying legal and tax measures that may serve as leverage for more donations. Moreover, committed individuals are supposed to be more loyal financiers than

NOTES

55
Interventions by Sigrid
HEMELS and Bert DEMARSIN.

56
Intervention by Ivo VAN
VAERENBERGH.

57
Interventions by Bart DE BAERE and
Griet LEBEER.

58
Cf also M. REYNEBEAU, "Speciaal
in kunstland", column in De
Standaard 9 February 2011,
www.standaard.be

59
A. KLAMER, [Lecture 22 February
2010], in Agentschap Kunsten en
Erfgoed, Over collecties, Brussels,
2010, p. 16. Comp. S. EGGERMONT,
"Meer transparantie tussen private
en publieke actoren", <H>ART
48, 2009.

public authorities or corporations. As such, attracting middle-class small patrons is as important as bonding with the few upper-class patrons.[55]

Some heritage and arts organisations participate in broader initiatives, such as www.testament.be, where not-for-profit organisations from all sectors apply for bequests. From that perspective, private patronage has become a market and heritage and arts organisations should pay attention to the differentiation of their products and services. One suggested option in this regard is to create a return on investment by negotiating advantage claims, such as a limited edition multiple of original works financed by a friends association of a museum.[56]

Heritage and arts organisations are, however, each other's competitors in their niche market. In the absence of any serious policy framework, they will not jointly build expertise in fundraising nor collaborate in canalising gifts to the best-placed organisation.

More importantly, heritage and arts organisations seem reluctant to participate in the patronage market because they consider it important not to reduce the bonding to fundraising and because they feel heritage and art, as public goods, are *per se* outside the market as they should be.[57] Culture is considered a societal activity and commitment.[58]

What has been set out here amounts to qualifying cultural heritage as *common* rather than as private or public good.[59] Here again, two extremes (public-private) need be reconciled to a middle position (commons). Nevertheless, it is clear that not-for-profit organisations may take up a more active role, following the example of the immovable heritage sector.

ART COLLECTIONS

There are a fair number of private collections of museal value (in part) in Flanders.[60] As opposed to other countries, and particularly Germany, the collectors are, however, quite reluctant to go public although they would

60
See in general F. SWENNEN and
A. NIJS, *Vermogensplanning
van particuliere
kunstverzamelingen*, Brussels,
Larcier, 2009.
Furthermore from a
managerial point of view:
A. DUMEZ, *Een verkennend
onderzoek naar de private
behoeften en het publieke
potentieel van particuliere
kunstverzamelingen in
Vlaanderen*, Thesis Master
Cultural Management
University of Antwerp, 94 p.;
2010 J. SCHRAUWEN, *De private
kunstverzamelaar presenteert:
aanzet tot business model
en potentieel als publieke
cultureel-erfgoedorganisatie*,
Thesis Master Cultural
Management University
of Antwerp, 2010, 101 p.;
I. VERMEERSCH, *De private
verzamelingen beeldende
kunst. De verzamelaar op
zoek naar een finaliteit*, Thesis
Master Cultural Management,
2004, 122 p.

61
Intervention by Joke
SCHRAUWEN.

62
Interventions by Walter
VANHAERENTS, Ivo VAN
VAERENBERGHand Sigrid HEMELS.

63
Intervention by
Wim LEDEGEN.

certainly be complementary to the public collections.
Some collectors choose not to go public anyhow. Maybe
their social responsibility to unlock public goods could be
stimulated.[61]

Collectors who already are convinced of their social
responsibility seem reticent on PPP projects for different
reasons.[62]
Firstly, some collectors fear losing their highly esteemed
flexibility in acquiring and operating their collections.
Secondly, private collectors feel insufficiently appreciated or
confided in by public actors, regarding the added value they
can offer.[63] This feeling is in line with the lack of bonding
mentioned earlier. PPP starts with a good understanding
between both private and public actors.
Thirdly, the financial crisis of 2008 has probably caused
some reticence.
Some collectors, such as Ivo Van Vaerenbergh, therefore
opt for hospitable yet limited access to their collection.
More importantly, some collectors deliberately choose not
to enter into a PPP project (in Belgium), but to operate
independently – e.g. the Vanmoerkerke Collection – or
in private-private partnership – e.g. the Vanhaerents Art
Collection and the Vervoordt Foundation. They want to
position themselves first before reaching out to the public
sector. A limited form of PPP might consist in giving works
on loan to public museums, e.g. by Johan and Monia
Warnez.

Private collectors have not (yet) associated into an interest
group. A representative body might serve to explain and
negotiate their concerns with public authorities and the
public sector alike. Their individualistic approach – often a
strength in acquiring the collection – is, however, a flaw in
this regard. As a result, there is no co-ordinated approach,
likewise to the piecemeal approach on the public side.

Regarding public collections, one of the major issues is the use of opportunities to unlock the works public museums keep in storage, while only displaying a very low percentage of works.

For the Royal Fine Arts Museum in Antwerp, this amounts to a 90 % storage / 10 % display ratio.[64] In the light of the closing of the museum for restoration in the 2010-2017 period, efforts have been made to promote the collection's mobility program, which consists of giving works on loan to smaller public museums.

The Antwerp contemporary art museum has collaborated with local cultural centres with a view to broadening public accessibility of the collection.[65]

Would it not be an option to explore the profitable exploitation of the collection, and to collaborate with private (not-for-profit) organisations, such as hospitals or schools, or even with individuals? Some public museums already organise art leases to the private market.[66]

Also, public-public partnerships to unlock the stock may serve to neutralise the Matthew effect, through which the renowned and popular museums attract all private patrons to the detriment of the smaller museums.[67] Distribution may thus be organised between the museums.

The unlocking of the stock must of course be compatible with the other functions of the museums, particularly research and preservation. The stock, even without being 'activated', also represents an option value.[68]

On various occasions,[69] proposals have been made to create a public-private *pool* of artworks, following the example of the current Flemish Art Collection website.[70] Digitalised archives and information would be operated by an independent foundation for both public and private partners; works should also be accessible or available for loan to the members.

NOTES

64
www.kmska.be (NL) > Collectie >
Kunst en mobiliteit.

65
E.g. M HKA in the VISITE project.
www.muhka.be> Shows > Visual
Art > 09.

66
http://www.bonnefanten.nl/en/
art_lease. Compare with the
private sector, e.g.
www.stima.be

67
Intervention by
Bert DEMARSIN.

68
Intervention by
Bart DE BAERE.

69
Intervention by Griet LEBEER, earlier
on the occasion of the Public
Private Paintings symposium in
Mu.ZEE on 9/10 December 2010
and before in P. DEPONDT, *Met
nieuwsgierige blik*, Brussels, ASP
Editions, 2010, p. 76 (interview
with Frederik Swennen).

70
www.vlaamsekunstcollectie.be

71
Explanatory Note, p. 15-16.
www.kunstenenerfgoed.be
> Agentschap > Wet- en
Regelgeving > Cultureel-
Erfgoeddecreet.

72
The Flemish Government
invited tenders for a
confidential research project
on the subject.

73
Intervention by
Fernand HUTS.

ART STORAGE

Regarding art storage, one may again distinguish between the 'hardware' – a secured and acclimatised building – and the 'software' – inventories and documentation, care and preservation, handling and moving. Simply put, one might say that the private market proportionally has more expertise on the hardware, whereas the public sector has the expertise on the software.

In the Explanatory Note on the Cultural Heritage Decree, the Flemish authorities have acknowledged the urgent need for high quality storage space for cultural heritage.[71] A policy to realise this, however, has to be developed on the provincial level. Research projects have been carried out with a view to mapping the needs.
Awaiting policy measures, some collaboration between public and private parties already exists.
On the one hand, the Flemish authorities – for their collections and those of the Flemish museums – and some museums have already concluded contracts on a case-by-case basis on storage with Katoen Natie as a private partner, in the form of rental agreements or service contracts.[72]
On the other hand, service contracts exist in which the private sector pays for public expertise on the management of stored private collections. For instance Fernand Huts is keen to collaborate with the Public sector.[73]

A coordinated approach of this collaboration is desirable and possible, for the multi-levelled public sector and a quickly changing private market to become equal partners. A win-win situation could be achieved in a participative PPP project where the private partner would contribute the hardware and the public sector the software. A return on investment for the private partner could lie in a concession for the operation of the storage spaces – through rental agreements – for both public and private clients. Clients could then opt for made-to-measure 'software' services, provided by the public partner. Besides revenue, a return on investment for the public partner would lie in the accessibility of private collections for research and, possibly, display. The Boijmans van Beuningen Museum in Rotterdam has already made proposals for such a project.[74] The municipal authorities have postponed the project, however and will rent storage space on the private market in the next 5 years.[75]

NOTES

ARTISTS' ARCHIVES

One of the operational objectives for the Cultural Policy 2010-2015 is specific support for artists' archives, and for building and sharing knowledge on their conservation, management and display & exhibition.[76] Digitalisation is also important in this regard.[77] The Flemish Assessment Committee for the Visual Arts has indeed noted that any Flemish policy in this regard is lacking, wrongly leaving the initiative to individual artists('estates).[78] Some artists[79] or artists' estates[80] have already received support in the form of project grants. Other artists('estates) aim for broader projects, which are difficult to fit into the current legal framework, however, particularly because of a risk of conflict of interests. Jef Geys' KODEC is presented as an example of a broader project hereafter (see p. 68-69). Awaiting the development of a policy, some opportunities for contractual collaboration – yes, even PPP – are to be found in loaning and licensing agreements with individual artists('estates). Yet a policy will be difficult to develop, since each artist would expect regard for the individuality of his or her archive or might wish not to be associated with other artists' archives.[81]

74
F. Swennen, "Deconstructing –
Reconstructing. PPP of Contemporary
Arts Organisations", www.bamart .be >
EN > Topics > Documentation (Report
of an Art Brussels 2010 Debate).

75
www.boijmans.nl> NL >Pers> Press
release of 12 October 2010.

76
Flemish Parliament 2009-2010, nr.
192/1, p. 29.

77
Intervention by An Moons.

78
"Landschapstekening Hedendaagse
Beeldende Kunst 2009", p. 21, www.
kunstenenerfgoed.be > NL > Beleid >
Landschapstekeningen.

79
Koen Broucke,
www.koenbroucke.be

80
The Maarten van Severen Foundation,
www.maartenvanseveren.be

81
L.-P. Van Eeckhoutte, "Juridische
mogelijkheden voor de ontsluiting
van kunstenaarsarchieven", [Research
paper University of Antwerp Law
Research School], 2010.

new opportunities

A — CONTEXT

/ TECHNIQUES

B — TAX

A — CONTEXT

NOTES

82
A. M. DRAYE, *De bescherming van het roerend en onroerend erfgoed*, Brussels, Larcier, 2007, 435 p.; F. JONGEN, "L'aide à l'activité artistique: interventions des pouvoirs publics et stimulation du soutien privé", *Ann. dr. Louv.* 1988, p. 443. For The Netherlands: I. VAN DER VLIES, *De kunst en het recht*, The Hague, Boom Juridische uitgevers, 2005.

83
www.cultuurinvest.be

84
Commission Regulation (EU) No. 731/2010 of 11 August 2010 concerning the classification of certain goods in the Combined Nomenclature, *OJ* L 214, 14.8.2010, p. 2.

85
M. ROWELL, *Brancusi v United States. The Historic Trial, 1928*, Vilo International, 1999.

86
Flemish Decree of 24 January 2003 on the protection of movable cultural heritage of exceptional importance.

87
Lecture by Sigrid HEMELS.

Public authorities unilaterally reach out in particular to private (individual or corporate) initiatives regarding cultural heritage by three means.[82]

Supporting measures are a first instrument. Traditionally, public authorities support private entities fulfilling functions of a cultural heritage or arts organisation via public subventions. However, one should also mention Cultuurinvest, which is a label of the Flemish Private Equity Fund supporting private initiatives in the culture industry.[83] Such support is dependent, among others, on good governance of the initiative.

Secondly, *stimulating measures* may be taken, e.g. favourable tax regimes. Such a regime may be dependent on conservation and restoration following the techniques proposed by the public authorities.
It seems, though, that not all contemporary art forms can be grasped by law: installations by Bill Viola and Dan Flavin were qualified as video reproducing apparatus, projectors, loudspeakers, DVD's resp. wall lighting fittings – subject to 15 % VAT and customs duty – and not sculptures – subject to 5 % VAT and no customs duty.[84] The case remarkably resembles Brancusi v United States, nullifying the qualification of Bird in Space as kitchen utensils and hospital supplies and not sculpture because it was no realistic representation of a bird.[85]

Finally there are *restraining measures*, e.g. property restrictions or even expropriation with a view to protecting the cultural heritage from export or deterioration.[86]

Some of the measures mentioned above are obviously only applicable to specific initiatives.
Indeed, many legal possibilities regarding PPP projects only apply to real estate projects, such as granting building rights or real rights. The same is true for subventions, e.g. for the urban development of former brownfields or for the restoration of protected monuments.
As mentioned before, the legislator's awareness of the need for specific measures regarding movable cultural heritage has only been raised more recently.

———————

To a large extent, however, the legislator has a margin of appreciation on which kind of measure he will opt for, which he must do in function of a policy. In this regard it is important again, to find the right balance.

Under certain circumstances a tax incentive will give better leverage than a direct subsidy,[87] e.g. with a view to creating commitment to a privately owned good or because of the lower cost of tax incentives than of direct subventions. As opposed to subventions, tax incentives also allow to create a bond between the public and heritage organisations. The donator himself will in this case choose which project he will support, rather than having the government choose for him with low transparency. The heritage organisation, on the other hand, needs to reach out and is accountable to its public, which becomes more visible than the taxpayer in general. This presupposes an adapted mindset, e.g. client satisfaction will become a goal.
In summary, a system of tax deductions would contribute to strengthening the financial and social basis of heritage and arts organisations.

B — **TAX**

NOTES

88
In general: F. DERÈME, *La fiscalité des œuvres d'art et antiquités*, Brussels, Larcier, 2004.

89
With regard to its purposes: S.J.C. HEMELS, *Door de muze omhelsd: een onderzoek naar de inzet van belastingsubsidies voor kunst en cultuur in Nederland*, Wolf Legal, Nijmegen, 2005.

90
F. SWENNEN and A. NIJS, *Vermogensplanning van particuliere kunstverzamelingen*, Brussels, Larcier, 2009, no. 41. Comp. for The Netherlands: F. GRAPPERHAUS and S. HEMELS, *Mecenaat en fiscus*, Deventer, Kluwer, 2010, p. 58.

91
L.-P. VAN EECKHOUTTE, "Juridische mogelijkheden voor de ontsluiting van kunstenaarsarchieven", [Research paper University of Antwerp Law Research School], 2010, p. 12.

92
A. VAN DE VOORDE, *Mark Eyskens. Een biografie*, Tielt, Lannoo, 2003, p. 266.

93
www.museemagrittemuseum.be

The use of tax incentives is an evergreen to attract additional private means, besides taxes, for the public sector.

Private initiatives to the benefit of the public cultural heritage are no exception to that rule.[88] Two incentives are traditionally applied. On the one hand, there are tax reductions or even exemptions for donations or bequests made to public cultural heritage organisations. On the other hand, donations to recognised organisations may be deduced from income before taxation.

More importantly, cultural goods are subject to an exceptional treatment.[89]

Firstly, not only donations of money but also donations of works of art, recognised to be of international fame or belonging to the national cultural heritage, to public authorities or museums, may be deduced from income before taxation.[90]

Secondly, works of arts – including libraries or archives[91] – recognised to be of international fame or belonging to the national cultural heritage may be given in payment of inheritance taxes. The so-called *Magritte Act* was designed in 1985 following the example of the French *Loi Malraux* of 1968 and adapted after the death of Georgette Magritte in 1987 with a view to avoiding the export of large parts of the archive and works René Magritte had left her. Her heirs would not have been able to pay the succession tax in money and would have had to sell archive and works. The heirs not coming to an agreement with the Belgian state after all, many parts of the inheritance were exported for

94
Cfin general: M. BETHENOD et al., *Propositions en faveur du développement du marché de l'art en France*, Proposition à la Ministre de la Culture et de la Communication, 2008, www.culture.gouv.fr

95
As defined in the Flemish Decree of 24 January 2003 on the protection of movable cultural heritage of exceptional importance.

96
Intervention by Marina LAUREYS.

97
Cp F. GRAPPERHAUS and S. HEMELS, *Mecenaat en fiscus*, Deventer, Kluwer, 2010, p. 59.

98
Lecture by Anne Mie DRAYE; cf also: A. M. DRAYE et al., *Studieopdracht naar de problematiek, mogelijkheden en opportuniteiten van de Vlaamse bevoegdheid op het vlak van successierechten, voor de collectieopbouw van de Vlaamse musea en erfgoedinstellingen en voor de collectie van de Vlaamse Gemeenschap*, Hasselt, 2006, 342 p., www.kunstenenerfgoed. be > Erfoed > Successierechten > Actueel.

99
Intervention by Sigrid HEMELS.

sale at Sotheby's in London.[92] It must be said, though, that the manager of the inheritance finally found an agreement with the Brussels Fine Arts Museum and a corporate patron with a view to creating the *Musée Magritte Museum*.[93]

———

Nevertheless, the current tax framework is considered inadequate for various reasons,[94] two of which may be mentioned here.

A first objection to the current framework is that it only allows transferring ownership from the private to the public sector and does not stimulate private initiatives. The means to at least partly leave control over, or use (e.g. usufruct) of, the works with the private party are fairly limited.
A research project has been carried out on tax incentives for privately owned cultural goods. One of the results is a proposal to (partly) exempt movable heritage of exceptional importance[95] from inheritance tax, so as to avoid export and to achieve conservation in good circumstances, while leaving the family in possession. The purpose of this exemption is to increase the number of protected movable heritage goods of exceptional importance.[96]
Of course, such public investment in privately owned goods presupposes a return.
This return may lie in making those goods partially public;[97] the rate of the exemption would indeed depend on the public accessibility of the cultural goods.[98]
In case the goods are not publicly accessible, the return on investment may lie in its non-use value. It is debatable, however, whether the public authorities should finance privately owned goods with non-use value as the sole counterpart, achieved through prohibiting export or subjecting it to a right of pre-emption and obliging good conservation and restoration. Use value abroad could then be the better option[99] if the return on investment for the public sector does not imply any consumption value.
All this may be nuanced if the public support serves another purpose too. The so-called Percentage Rule obliges a

decreasing percentage of the (re)building cost of buildings for public services to be spent on integrated works of art by living artists.[100] Moreover, private corporations are allowed tax depreciation of *not* publicly accessible integrated works of art by artists residing in Belgium.[101] This is clearly a form of indirect subventions to artists. Besides, some employers used this measure for the cultural education and satisfaction of their employees. The integration of works of art by *De Nieuwe Visie* in the textile company *Dulcia* was very renowned.[102]

A second objection aims to broaden the scope of the tax incentives.

On various occasions a testator has expressed the wish to come to an agreement with tax services *during his life* on which works may be given in payment after his death. One could also consider applying the system of incentives to other tax regimes. One could for instance allow works of art to be given in payment for other than inheritance taxes. Another option would be to increase the incentive. A first example is to increase the percentage of the income one is allowed to donate with deduction before taxation. A second example is to allow deduction of personal or corporate investments in recognised cultural private equity funds.[103] A third example is to create additional tax shelters for investments in cultural goods. A tax shelter could allow a person to deduct more than 100 % of a donation from his taxable income. It could allow corporations to deduct more than 100 % of their investments in heritage projects from their taxable income – the current film tax shelter allows a 150 % deduction.[104] It could finally allow the heirs to deduct more than 100 % of the value of the works of art from inheritance tax, which is already possible in The Netherlands.[105]

NOTES

100
Decree of 23 December 1986 on the integration of works of art in buildings used for public services or assimilated services and of subsidised establishments, associations and institutes of the Flemish Community.

101
Administrative Commentary of the Income Tax Code 1992, art.61/233, www.fisconet.be

102
K. De Wolf, *Kunst in de fabriek. De Nieuwe Visie van Beervelde tot Dulcia*, Ghent, Stichting Mens & Cultuur, s.d.

103
F. Grapperhaus and S. Hemels, *Mecenaat en fiscus*, Deventer, Kluwer, 2010, p. 44.

104
T. Spaas and K. Roelands, "Beleggen in de film-tax shelter", *Estate Planning Journal* (B) 2009-3, p. 179.

105
F. Grapperhaus and S. Hemels, *Mecenaat en fiscus*, Deventer, Kluwer, 2010, p. 15.

/ CONCLUSIONS

At the expert seminar on 21 December 2010, many
participants were excited to find all stakeholders around
the table. That feeling was significant in a negative sense; it
illustrated that PPP on cultural heritage is at an early stage,
if not inexistent.
Encounters between public and private partners on cultural
heritage up to now have been mostly limited to one-way
traffic, consisting of the imposition of regulations by the
public sector, and of patronage by the private sector.

_____

NOTES

106
Intervention by Fernand Huts.

107
Lecture by Sigrid Hemels. Also
see www.cultuurmecenaat.nl

108
E.g. Centrum Geef om Cultuur
(www.reneesteenbergen.com)

109
L.-P. Van Eeckhoutte,
"Juridische mogelijkheden
voor de ontsluiting van
kunstenaarsarchieven",
[Research paper University of
Antwerp Law Research School],
2010, p. 19.

110
Intervention
by Marina Laureys.

111
Intervention
by Jan Rombouts.

112
Cf in general: A. Klamer et al.,
*Financing the arts and culture in
the European Union,* Study for
the European Parliament, DG
Internal Policies of the Union,
2006, IP/B/CULT/ST/2005_104.
Cf also www.academiavitae.org
> Creative Financing of the Arts
Symposium.

A first stage of (further) development of public private
encounters is to creatively give substance to new one-way
shifts of resources, e.g. with the help of Flanders DC.

A possible contribution from the private sector has
been summarised slogan-like as "unlocking the blocked
potential"[106] of the publicly owned and operated cultural
heritage. It particularly consists of using managerial and
marketing strategies of the private market in the public
sphere. Talent management, with the use of incentives,
for instance, is an important lever to stimulate commitment
by employees to 'their' cultural heritage project. As such,
one should support the empowerment of the public
sector to apply private sector techniques of 'cultural
entrepreneurship'[107], with a view to at least realising more
private support.[108] This may be achieved through patronage
of competence (*mécénat de compétence*).[109]

Besides the provision of cultural goods, an important
contribution by the public sector would be the provision of
the broad expertise in its operation.

Thirdly, there have always been friends' associations,
long-term loans by private collectors and sponsorship by
corporations.[110] The mixed financing techniques of heritage
and the arts to which these forms of collaboration lead,
may be called the Third Way.[111] They may and should be
modernised now, in the light of PPP. One example is the

113
Intervention by
Wim LEDEGEN.

114
Intervention by
Steven VAN GARSSE.

115
Intervention by
Ellen LOOTS.

116
Intervention by
Steven VAN GARSSE.

117
Interventions by Sigrid HEMELS
and Walter VANHAERENTS.

118
Lecture by
Anne Mie DRAYE.

use of (tax incentives for) interest-free loans (warranted by a public party).[112]

_____

As mentioned before, the mere shift of resources is not PPP. Yet PPP in general has emerged from attempts to increase efficiency in the public sector, particularly the efficient use of public resources.

Indeed, creative one-way shifts of resources are an indispensible first step to subsequently realising a PPP mindset.[113] One should focus on the current collaborations and develop best practices on this basis[114] before going further.[115]

_____

Regarding PPP on cultural heritage, we have seen that projects up to now have implied private investments in publicly owned immovable heritage, in return for a profitable exploitation of real estate. A comparable return on investment is hard to realise in projects on movable cultural heritage or the arts. New instruments need to be developed to realise this; the potential for their use is thought to be present.[116] Nevertheless, such instruments will remain unused in the absence of movable heritage and the arts becoming more appealing to a broader private public. A stronger bond between the public and the private is necessary. An important issue in this regard is the recognition by the public sector of private parties as their peers in responsibility for cultural heritage and the arts,[117] even if their perspective is different.

Attention must be paid in particular to public investments in privately owned heritage, in return for their preservation in good circumstances and their accessibility. Private owners are often good owners – sometimes better than public owners – and should be stimulated in their committed ownership.[118] Moreover, the public authorities do not have the

45

financial strength to monopolise ownership and operation of cultural heritage. Institutions that used to be mainly subsidised, become more and more dependent on private patrons. It may be more interesting for the public authorities to support these initiatives as private initiatives rather than to take over ownership and operation.

I think, however, that heritage organisations must not be made dependent upon private patrons alone. Each heritage and arts organisation should be guaranteed a minimal free space with corresponding subventions,[119] on which it is not accountable to the public. Public authorities could provide the hardware and a basis for the software to which the private sector may subsequently contribute. Anyhow, it is easier for organisations to generate patronage for specific objects than for the abstract operation of the organisation.[120] A further extended privatisation may endanger the public good character of culture.[121]

Some stakeholders are already convinced of the sense of further developing PPP.[122] I, too, am enthusiastic about the opportunities.
Because cultural heritage and the arts are public goods, I am convinced that the public authorities should take the lead, which they currently fail to do. What they are doing, may be too little, too late.[123] The multi-levelled organisation of competences in cultural heritage is not sufficient as an excuse in this regard.
At the very least a – public-private – foundation might be created to advise the different partners in the absence of a coordinated policy.[124] Politicians, take the lead; the others will follow.

NOTES

117
Interventions by Sigrid HEMELS and
Walter VANHAERENTS.

118
Lecture by Anne Mie DRAYE.

119
K. STRUBBE, "Het gat in onze cultuur",
column in De Standaard 7 February
2011, www.standaard.be

120
Cp F. GRAPPERHAUS and S. HEMELS,
Mecenaat en fiscus, Deventer, Kluwer,
2010, p. 18.

121
M. REYNEBEAU, "Speciaal in kunstland",
column in De Standaard 9 February
2011, www.standaard.be

122
S. EGGERMONT, "Meer transparantie
tussen private en publieke actoren",
<H>ART # 48, 2009.

123
P. DEPONDT, Met nieuwsgierige blik,
Brussels, ASP Editions, 2010, p. 71
ff (Collectioneur meet polsslag van
de tijd).

124
Cp on the Prins Bernhard Cultuurfonds
in The Netherlands: F. GRAPPERHAUS
and S. HEMELS, Mecenaat en fiscus,
Deventer, Kluwer, 2010, p. 6.

/ ANNEXES

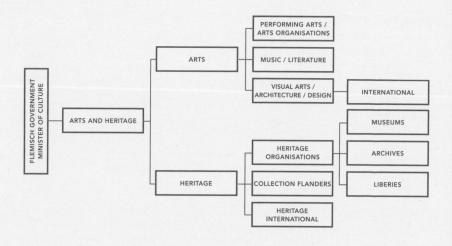

ARTS & HERITAGE: THE PUBLIC SECTOR

For the Flemish (Cultural)
Community in Belgium, he Flemish
Government is substantially
responsible for supporting and
protecting arts and heritage.

ARTS

Subventions are available for
organisations, artists, publications and
recording projects.
Organisations may be supported
for their operation and for specific
projects.

HERITAGE

Heritage organisations can be
awarded a *quality label*. Besides,
support may be granted for the
operation, for employment, for
projects, to heritage covenants with
provinces and communes, and for
publications.
The Collection Flanders team is
responsible for the Flemish art
collection (Collection Flanders), for
the protection of cultural heritage of
exceptional importance and for the
permits to export cultural heritage
objects (see p. 38).

For the above, an *arts organisation* is
any organisation that creates, presents
and/or has a focus on a public.
Museums, archives and libraries may
be recognised as a *cultural heritage
organisation* – with a quality label
– in case they fulfil the four ICOM-
functions (collect, preserve, research
and display).

www.kunstenenerfgoed.be

Besides, the **Federal Belgian
authorities** remain competent with
regard so some tax measures, e.g. the
decision on the payment of succession
taxes with works of art (see p. 40-41).

On a lower level, the **provinces**
and **communes** are also directly
or indirectly (via subventions by the
Flemish and/or Provincial level)
obliged to develop a policy regarding
arts and heritage.

That multi-levelled public
organisation (see p. 18) is subject
to relevant supranational and
international rules as well.

Vlaamse overheid

RELEVANT ORGANISATIONS

FLEMISH PPP KNOWLEDGE CENTRE

Mid-2002, the Flemish Government established the Flemish PPP Knowledge Centre, in order to boost the introduction and implementation of PPP in Flanders.
In compliance with the Better Administrative Policy operation, the Knowledge Centre is part of the policy area "Services for the General Government Policy of the Flemish Authorities", as part of the entity "Flemish Government Executive Staff".
The Flemish PPP Knowledge Centre is the junction and network organisation par excellence of and for the Flemish authorities, which advises and inspires the PPP policy, and supports public private partnership projects in Flanders.
In order to realise social added value and efficiency gain, the Flemish PPP Knowledge Centre actively unites the following four functions:

_ field developer
_ knowledge broker
_ process guide
_ added value monitor

In its capacity of **field developer**, the knowledge centre provides both the Flemish government and the private sector with information on the PPP policy and PPP possibilities. It tries to promote the PPP self-reliance of these parties.

As **knowledge broker**, the knowledge centre assumes an advisory role (both policy-wise and project-wise) and collects and shares PPP knowledge, experiences and models with all parties involved. Shortening the PPP learning curve for Flanders is a clear objective.

The **process guidance function** comprises the provision of advice and guidance to the Flemish public administration in the detection of potential PPP projects and the design of these projects. The knowledge centre will not coordinate any projects itself. This remains a task of the responsible administration. However, the centre is involved in the preparation of a PPP construction, and will guide the PPP process.

Finally, the knowledge centre also assumes the role of **added value monitor** by evaluating the added value of a public private partnership.

FLANDERS DISTRICT OF CREATIVITY

Flanders DC is the Flemish organisation for entrepreneurial creativity, established by the Flemish Government. Flanders DC's mission is to make entrepreneurial Flanders more creative and to make creative Flanders more entrepreneurial. This is not an end in itself but a means to preserve our prosperity and create new jobs.

As a consequence Flanders DC builds knowledge, raises awareness and designs useful tools for anyone wishing to launch a creative and enterprising project and targets entrepreneurs, teachers, students, policy-makers and the general public.

Flanders Fashion Institute (FFI) is part of Flanders DC and encourages entrepreneurship in the fashion industry in Flanders, assists designers in their careers and promotes Flemish fashion in Belgium and abroad.

More information:
www.flandersdc.be - www.flandersdc.be/blog

Vlaams
Kenniscentrum
PPS

INSPIRING CREATIVITY

RELEVANT ORGANISATIONS

CULTUURINVEST

Leverage For Innovative
Entrepreneurs And A New
Generation Of Investors

Information For The Cultural
Entrepreneur

Solid Investments In Creativity

Creative companies that are active in
the arts or design often face hardship
in finding risk capital for further
growth. Most venture capitalists
do not want to take a leap of faith
and invest in companies which
they consider too risky or having
insufficient profit potential. These
prejudices often stem from their lack
of affinity with the cultural sector.

CultuurInvest, an investment fund
for the Flemish cultural industries
managed by ParticipatieMaatschappij
Vlaanderen (PMV), wants to bridge
this gap between the arts and the
economy. *CultuurInvest* aims at
providing creative companies access
to venture capital. In this way it
wants to create leverage for structural
growth and professionalism.

CultuurInvest has been initiated by the
Flemish government and is being
operated by PMV.

WHAT DOES
CULTUURINVEST OFFER?

CultuurInvest may, depending on the
growth phase and the exact needs of
your company, invest in two ways:

1. Private equity A venture capital
investment in more mature start-
up companies by means of share
ownership.

2. Subordinated debt long-term loans,
possibly to be converted in shares

CultuurInvest may equally facilitate
access to financing by referring you
to Vinnof, the Flemish innovation
fund, or Waarborgregeling, both
products of ParticipatieMaatschappij
Vlaanderen (PMV). Private investors
or the Federal Participation Fund may
also be interested in you.

CultuurInvest does not invest in cultural
organizations that receive subsidies in
a structural manner from the Flemish
government. *CultuurInvest* does not
hand out grants or subsidies. The
fund invests risk capital in companies
and wants to get financial return on
its investments.

WHO CAN APPLY?

To be eligible for an investment by
CultuurInvest, your company has to
offer high-quality cultural products
and/or services that possess an
obvious market potential.

The following sectors are specifically
targeted:

_ new media and computer games
_ the audiovisual sector and digital design
_ the musical industry and concerts
_ design and designer fashion
_ printed media and graphic design
_ publishing and bookshops
_ musicals and theatrical arts
_ fine art distribution
_ etc.

RELEVANT ORGANISATIONS

CULTUURINVEST

THE INVESTMENT PROCESS

Investment Proces	
1	**e-Application** — You can make your pitch on www.cultuurinvest.be and convince us of the potential of your product and your market approach.
2	**Intake - interview** — Together, we investigate whether your application fulfills the basic criteria of a sound investment.
3	**Intensive analysis** — Together, we analyze the elements of your business plan. We greatly value entrepreneurship and the way you want to approach the market.
4	**Conditional Offer** — We discuss what type of financing your company needs, depending on your needs and your growth stage. We make you an offer.
5	**Investment Committee** — A specialized committee decides autonomously to invest or not to invest.
6	**Investment** — We draw up a contract which is signed by all parties concerned. We offer you a glass of champagne to celebrate our partnership.
	Monitoring & Coaching — You report to us on the realization of your business plan. Within our network and know how we can coach your managementskills.

Repayment - Exit

ANALYZING YOUR BUSINESSPLAN

In order to be eligible for an investment, you must possess a convincing business plan, or we help you in drawing one up. *CultuurInvest* will then analyze and discuss this plan with you. In this way we become real partners in giving your company all strategic chances for success.

WHERE CAN YOU FIND MORE INFORMATION?

If you want to appeal to *CultuurInvest* for the financing of your company, or if you just want to check out your options, please contact *CultuurInvest* at cultuurinvest@pmv.eu

More information on our financial products for small and medium-sized enterprises may be found at www.pmv. eu, your guide in public financing. This Dutch language website also features a number of leaflets about the products PMV offers to entrepreneurs: CultuurInvest, Vinnof, Waarborgregeling, ARKimedes. These may be downloaded or you can ask for a printed copy.

CultuurInvest
Oude Graanmarkt 63
1000 Brussel
cultuurinvest@pmv.eu
www.cultuurinvest.be
www.pmv.eu

RELEVANT ORGANISATIONS

KING BAUDOUIN FOUNDATION

FACILITATING THE PRESERVATION OF OUR HERITAGE

Those concerned with the preservation of our heritage can count on the Foundation to provide advice and support for their project.

The policy of preserving major elements of our heritage pursued by the Foundation for nearly 25 years has secured a very special place for it in this field. As a private institution acting on behalf of all, the Foundation is uniquely positioned to establish a link between private initiatives and public institutions. It can react rapidly and flexibly and is always ready to serve the community.

In accordance with what are often the precise wishes of art patrons, it provides customised approaches that have long proven their worth. Anyone who owns a collection or a major work of art, or a person of means who wishes to make a bequest in the public interest, is faced with questions and uncertainties. The work of a lifetime cannot be relegated to an uncertain future. The owner of a major item of our heritage often has a sense of special responsibility to future generations – so he wants to be sure that his decision and philosophy will be duly respected.

It is at times difficult, when in search of advice on such matters, to get an overview of the various alternatives and to assess their advantages and disadvantages. It is usually easier to find a solution by turning to an external and impartial partner. The Foundation's extensive network and knowledge of the relevant legislation are indispensable for seeing this type of project through. Thanks to its flexible approaches and unrelenting attention to changes in society, the Foundation can approach several partners as and when necessary or proceed with the selected partner, if the right opportunities arise.

HERITAGE FUND

The preservation of our heritage has been an overriding priority of the Heritage Fund since 1987. The Fund acquires major works, documents and collections. It also accepts bequests with immense gratitude. The Fund Management Committee has an annual budget of € 600.000 to acquire items that come on the art market in Belgium or abroad or which are offered for sale directly by a private owner. This sum can also be used to enhance bequeathed artworks. The Fund has thus managed to amass a collection of nearly 5,000 works of art and 5 major archives – all of which are accessible in more than 20 museums and cultural institutions throughout the country.

King Baudouin
Foundation
Working together for a better society

RELEVANT ORGANISATIONS

PHILANTHROPY

Art patrons share the Foundation's concern to preserve our heritage and have turned to it to see their project through. More than 30 funds are already active, representing a budget of € 1.200.000 in 2010.

The needs and scope of action are varied. Potential donors may decide to keep major specimens such as an art collection, a historical building or a natural heritage item. They may also wish to attract a specific target group's interest in our heritage or to support the restoration of significant elements of our movable and architectural heritage.

Through its diverse range of activities the Heritage Fund has acquired a global view of respective needs and requirements. It can propose cooperation between the different registered funds so as to optimise their impact. Maximising philanthropic projects is another characteristic of the Fund's role as a facilitator.

LIST OF PARTICIPANTS TO THE EXPERT
SEMINAR ON 21 DECEMBER 2010

Bart De Baere M HKA / **Isabelle De Baets** <H>ART / **Bert Demarsin** Katholieke Universiteit Leuven, Art, Law & Management Research Programme) / **Camille Depuydt** Katoen Natie / Prof. dr. **ANNE MIE DRAYE** is full professor of law at the Universiteit Hasselt, Faculty of Law and associate professor of law at the Katholieke Universiteit Leuven. She is president of the Royal Commission of Monuments and Landscapes. She introduced the power session on legal techniques of PPP / **Sam Eggermont** BAM - Instituut voor Beeldende, Audiovisuele en mediakunst / **Hans Feys** Agentschap Kunsten en Erfgoed / Prof. dr. dr. h. c. mult. **BRUNO S. FREY** is currently distinguished professor at the University of Warwick and full professor at the University of Zürich, Institute for Empirical Research in Economics. He is a honorary doctor at the University of Aix-en-Provence (2010), the Free University Brussels (2009), the University of Göteborg (1998) and the University of St Gallen (1998). He addressed the audience in a keynote lecture with thoughts by a cultural economist / Prof dr. **SIGRID HEMELS** is professor of tax law at the Erasmus University Rotterdam - Erasmus School of Law and Senior Professional Support Lawyer Tax at Allen & Overy. She introduced the power session on tax instruments / **Fernand Huts** Katoen Natie / **Marina Laureys** Agentschap Kunsten en Erfgoed / **Griet Lebeer** freelance adviser / **Wim Ledegen** Katoen Natie / **Ellen Loots** University of Antwerp, Department of Management (Cultural Management) / **An Moons** Cabinet provincial representative for culture, Limburg & Free University Brussels / **Jan Rombouts** City of Antwerp / Prof. dr. **ANNICK SCHRAMME** is associate professor at the University of Antwerp, Department of Management (Cultural Management) and coordinator of the Master in cultural management. She is expert at the cabinet of the city representative for culture / **Joke Schrauwen** Universiteit Antwerpen, departement Management (Cultuurmanagement) / **Dirk Snauwaert** Wiels / Prof. dr. mr. **FREDERIK SWENNEN** is associate professor at the University of Antwerp, University of Antwerp Law Research School, attorney at the Brussels bar (Greenille) and coordinator of Stew-art by Greenille, legal office for art collectors / **Ernest Van Buynder** President of the friends of the M HKA / **Louis-Philippe Van Eeckhoutte** University of Antwerp Law Research School / **Steven Van Garsse** Flemish Knowledge Centre PPP / **Kit Van Gestel** Public Management Institute, Katholieke Universiteit Leuven / **Katrijn Van Kerchove** Agentschap Kunsten en Erfgoed / **Ivo Van Vaerenbergh** Board of directors M HKA / **Hélène Vandenberghe** Estate Philippe Vandenberg / **Walter Vanhaerents** Vanhaerents Art Collection / **Niek Verslype** Greenille attorneys/ **Sophie Vigneron** Kent Law School / **Jeroen Walterus** FARO - Vlaams steunpunt voor Cultureel erfgoed.

/ CASES — PORTRAITS

QUEENS

REMBRANDT HARMENSZ. VAN RIJN, BELSHAZZAR'S FEAST — C. 1636

MANE, THECEL, PHARES:
contemporary art is an economic bubble — see p. 21

PAOLO VERONESE, THE WEDDING AT CANA — 1562-1563

Why is a damaged painting, on display in the Louvre and not
in its original setting, attractive? — see p. 21

/ **CASES**

63

Marcel Broodthaers' Grande Casserole de Moules was acquired in 2001 by SMAK in Ghent through various popular fundraising activities — see p. 28

MARCEL BROODTHAERS, GRANDE CASSEROLE DE MOULES — 1966

Following the closure of the Saint-Nicolas d'Oignies Priory, it was the Congregation of the Sisters of Notre-Dame de Namur who selflessly and devotedly took care of the conservation and display of the Treasure of Oignies from 1818 to 2010. In 2010, the recently-listed Treasure was handed over to the King Baudouin Foundation, which now makes it accessible to the general public, in collaboration with the Province of Namur, the Archaeological Society of Namur and the French Community — see p. 26 and 52

65

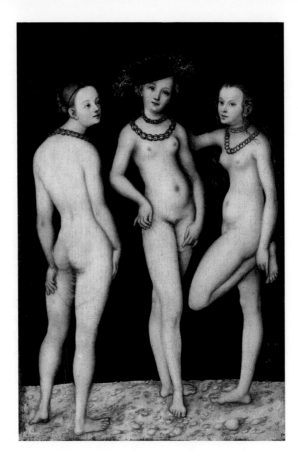

In 2010-2011, the Louvre in Paris received € 1 million from 5.000 patrons for the acquisition of Lucas Cranach's The Three Graces (1531) (www.troisgraces.fr). It now appeals to Dutch patrons in particular with a view of acquiring Frans Hals' Portrait of a Man — see p. 29

TITIAN, DIANA AND ACTAEON — 1556-1559

Titian's Diana and Actaeon (1556-1559) was on loan at the
National Gallery, London in 2008 when the Duke of Sutherland
decided to sell it. The National Galleries of Scotland and the
National Gallery, London successfully appealed for £ 50 million
in a fundraising campaign — see p. 29

68

The Palazzo Fortuny is operated through a
PPP-project between the Fondazione Musei Civici
di Venezia and the Belgian Vervoordt Foundation.
A new exhibition will be organised during the 2011
Venice Biennale, under the title TRA. Edge of
Becoming — see p. 29

VIEW OF THE EXHIBITION 'IN-FINITUM' IN THE VENETIAN PALAZZO FORTUNY — 2009

The NeuesMuseumWeserburg in Bremen was founded in 1988 by the City of Bremen, the Kunstverein Bremen and some private collectors. The building is publicly owned, whereas the museum's collection exclusively consists of privately owned objects. A selection of the Vanhaerents Art Collection was part of the collection between 1991 and 1997 — see p. 29

NEUESMUSEUMWESERBURG, BREMEN

KEMPENS
Informatieblad

Verantwoordelijke
uitgever
JEF GEYS
Langvennen 79
2490 Balen
België
December 2010

SPECIALE EDITIE KODEC

Wij zoeken partners om onder de vorm van een publieke-private samenwerking dit project gestalte te geven.
Inlichtingen: jan.devree@muhka.be

We are seeking partners for a public-private cooperation, in order to make this project happen.
Info: jan.devree@muhka.be

On est à la recherche de partenaires enfin de realiser ce projet sous forme publique-privé.
Informations: jan.devree@muhka.be

Some artists' projects are difficult to
fit into the current legal framework, that
lacks creativity — see p. 34

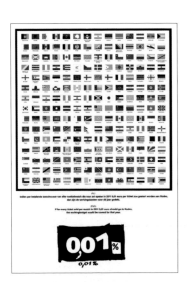

"Six circular fluorescent lighting tubes and six lighting fittings of plastics to be fixed to the wall and operated according to instructions by the artist do not qualify as sculpture, as it is not the installation that constitutes a 'work of art' but the result of the operations (the light effect) carried out by it. Neither is it a collector's piece of historical interest." The products must be classified as wall lighting fittings, according to the European Commission in 2010 — see p. 38

DAN FLAVIN, UNTITLED (TO A MAN, GEORGE MCGOVERN) — 1972

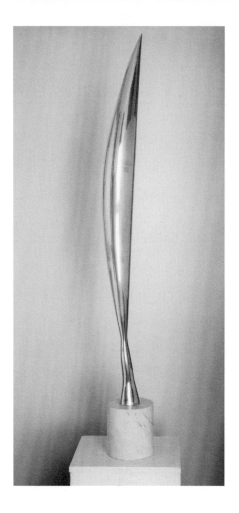

In 1926, Marcel Duchamp escorted Brancusi's Bird in Space to New York, for an exhibition. Upon disembarkment from the Paris, the US Customs classified the work as "Kitchen utensils and hospital supplies" and not as sculpture, for the work did not realistically represent a bird. The Court however overruled that decision: abstract sculptures may qualify as art — see p. 38

CONSTANTIN BRANCUSI, BIRD IN SPACE — 1925-1926

/ PORTRAITS

Ivo Van Vaerenbergh is an entrepreneur. He is a member of the Royal Flemish Academy of Belgium for Sciences and the Arts, Director of the Board of the Brussels Philharmonic and of M HKA, Museum of Contemporary Art Antwerp. He restored and lives in an 18th century Cistercian priory, a classified monument. Cistercian architecture and art was characterised by its simplicity and austerity. In contrast to the richly carved capitals and portals at other monasteries, Cistercian art was minimal, with almost no figurative carvings to distract the monks. As an art collector for more than forty years and keeping with the values of the order of the Cistercians, his collection is mostly minimal. As the landscape is also a great part of the appeal of Cistercian monasteries, land art is also found in the listed park. Ivo Van Vaerenbergh offers hospitable but limited access to his collection — see p. 31

IVO VAN VAERENBERGH

WALTER VANHAERENTS

Walter Vanhaerents is former CEO of
Vanhaerents NV. He started collecting contemporary
art 30 years ago. In 2006, a structure for the
collection was set up in which the collector's son and
daughter participate, with a view of guaranteeing
the collection's continuity. Subsequently, the
VanhaerentsArtCollection was given its own
premises in Brussels. Each three years, a large
collection presentation is set up. Besides, there are
smaller exhibitions. The collection is open for group
visits. The second collection presentation will open
on the occasion of Art Brussels 2011, under the title
'Sympathy for the devil' — see p. 29 and 31

www.vanhaerentsartcollection.com

BIBL.

W. VANHAERENTS (ed.), *Disorder in the house*,
Lannoo, Tielt, 2010 (edited on the occasion of the first
collection presentation.)

Mark Vanmoerkerke (1952) started collecting contemporary art in 1998. What started as a decoration problem has grown into a passion. The Vanmoerkerke Collection holds post-conceptual art from European and American artists. Four years ago, the collection moved to a renovated industrial building in Ostend; two years later a new building was added to form the current home of the collection. The art space also acts as office space for Mark Vanmoerkerke's professional activities.

Twice a year, an independent curator is given the liberty to present work from the collection in both art spaces. Past curators include Peter Doroshenko, Robert Nickas, Anselm Franke and Jan Hoet. The collection can be visited by appointment only
— see p. 31

www.artcollection.be

MARK VANMOERKERKE

BORIS AND AXEL VERVOORDT

Axel Vervoordt (Antwerp, 1947) is an eclectic collector, tastemaker, and passionate uomo universalis whose quest for art and antiques made him one of the world's youngest and most driven dealers when he started his art and antiques business in the 1970s. The success of curated art presentations led Axel Vervoordt to embark upon an exhibition trilogy as of 2007, which took the art world by storm and made him finally decide to establish his Foundation.

The management of the Axel Vervoordt company, which oversees the array of services offered including art and antiques, home design and real estate, is gradually being taken over by his son Boris Vervoordt (Antwerp, b. 1974). Boris subtly led the way to reinforcing the company's strong image internally and externally as well as sharpening attention to the core group of art collecting clients. As of January 2011, Boris opened the Axel Vervoordt Gallery, located in the historical heart of Antwerp, the medieval street called 'Vlaeykensgang', that his father, Axel, revitalised in the late 60's.

The Vervoordt Foundation is the custodian of an art collection comprising of antiquities as well as contemporary works and further also assumes curatorial and educational activities. Currently based in Kanaal, a 19th century reconverted industrial site near Antwerp, the Foundation will eventually be housed in its own Museum which will be located on the same site
— see p. 29 and 31

www.axel-vervoordt.com

BIBL

AXEL VERVOORDT. *The Story of a Style, Assouline*, 2001, reprint 2008 (available in English, French, Dutch)
Artempo. Where Time Becomes Art, MER, 2007 (available in English and Italian)
Academia. Qui es-tu?, MER, 2008 (available in English and French)
In-finitum, MER, 2009 (available in English and Italian)
Wabi inspirations, Flammarion, November 2010 (available in English, French, Dutch, Italian and German)
Jef Verheyen. Le peintre flamant, published on the occasion of the exhibition Jef Verheyen and friends, Langen Foundation, Neuss, Germany, 11 September 2010 – 16 January 2011, ASA Publishers, 2010.

JOHAN DELCOUR AND MONIA WARNEZ

Johan Delcour and **Monia Warnez** are the founders
of Fotorama, specialised in digitalising art and fine
art printing. The JoMo Art Collection started in 2005
focused on young contemporary art.
Works from the collection are often lent in the context of
exhibitions worldwide. As curators they were responsible
for the exhibition 'Amusez Vous' (Berlin, 2008) about
the meaning of entertainment in our present society
and 'Tool' for the international Fotofestival (Knokke-
Heist, 2010) in which artists reflect on the illusion which
is created by the commercial industry. As the Belgian
part of the 'Young Collectors' project (Groningen, 2010)
a selection of their collection was exhibited in a solo
show. Since 2011, they give young artists a platform to
show their work in a daily life context with the Fotorama
window project stART — see p. 31

Fernand Huts, president of the Katoen Natie group, and his wife Karine, vice-president, love art.

The collection contains textiles and other artefacts from the late Egyptian period and modern and contemporary art from Europe and Latin America. The collection can be visited at the HeadquARTers of Katoen Natie in Antwerp where art, culture, architecture and tradition form part of day-to-day life. In HeadquARTers they organised an exhibition of Coptic, Islamic and Central-Asian textiles and artefacts. Three new exhibition rooms will be opened in October 2011 — see p. 33

caroline.dekyndt@katoennatie.com

BIBL.

A. DE MOOR, C. VERHECKEN-LAMMENS, A. VERHECKEN, *3500 years of textile art*, Lannoo, Tielt, 2010.

FERNAND HUTS

Frederik Swennen is associate professor of law at the University of Antwerp, where he holds the chair in the Law of Persons and Family Law. In addition, his research and education projects include Art & Law. He is a member of several academic committees and (editorial) boards and has written numerous academic publications in his fields of research and expertise.

As an attorney at Greenille and at Stew-art by Greenille, Frederik Swennen specializes in family law and in the legal unburdening of property and transfer of art collections and archives, on behalf of private and public parties.

COLOPHON / ©

© PHOTOGRAPHY

p. 58-59
Photo: Kristjan Kasikov © 2007

p. 63
Collectie S.M.A.K., Gent
Photo: Dirk Pauwels
© SABAM 2011

p. 65
Musée du Louvre, Paris
© RMN/Stéphane Maréchalle

p. 66-67
Photo: Peter Macdiarmid
© Getty Images

p. 72
Collectie Van Abbemuseum,
Eindhoven
Photo: Peter Cox, Eindhoven

p. 73
Los Angeles County Museum of Art
(LACMA)
© 2011. Digital Image Museum
Associates/LACMA/Art Resource
NY/Scala, Florence

p. 68
Photo: Jean-Pierre Gabriel
Second Floor with the following
works: `
Yves Klein (1928–1962)
Monochrome, 1956
Piero Manzoni (1933–1963)
Linea infinita, Collection of
seven boxes containing the Linea
finita, 1959
Floor lamps designed by Mario
Fortuny (1871–1949)
Natvar Bhasvar (1934)
Abdhee, 2006
Jef Verheyen (1932–1984)
Brazilië, 1968
Isamu Noguchi (1904–1988)
Wind Catcher, 1982
Alighiero Boetti (1940–1994)
Niente da vedere, niente da nascere
(Nothing to see, nothing to hide),
1969-86
Donald Judd (1928–1994)
Untitled, 1988

p. 88
Courtesy the artist,
Aliceday Brussels and Collectie
Frederik Swennen

AUTHOR
Frederik Swennen

PHOTOGRAPHY
Nicol'Andrea
www.nicolandrea.com

GRAPHIC DESIGN
Sven Beirnaert
www.svenbeirnaert.be

THANK YOU
Roel Mattheeuws, Alain Nijs,
Goedele Nuyttens, Annick Schramme,
Joke Schrauwen,
Louis-Philippe Van Eeckhoutte

PUBLISHER
University Press Antwerp
UPA is an imprint of Academic and
Scientific Publishers (ASP)
www.aspeditions.be

—

ISBN 978 90 5487 896 4
Legal Deposit: D/2011/11.161/059

SPONSOR

STEW▲RT
BY GREENILLE

Stew-art by Greenille is a legal office for art. As a
steward, it is specialized in the legal unburdening
of art-related questions. Stew-art by Greenille
assists artists, collectors and their estates, including
their relations with institutions that acquire,
conserve, research, communicate or exhibit art. It
offers A to Z legal support in acquiring, managing
and transferring art. Stew-art by Greenille selects
the form and synergy most appropriate to reach
dynamics and dynastics. Stew-art is a Greenille
label.

www.stew-art.eu
www.greenille.eu

TO WHOM IT MAY CONCERN

Walter Swennen, Bras d'honneur 2,
Oil on wood, 2007